Screws

Teaching Tips

Green Level 5

This book focuses on the phoneme **/ew/**.

Before Reading

- Discuss the title. Ask readers what they think the book will be about. Have them briefly explain why.
- Ask readers to look at the pictures on page 3. Sound out the objects' names together. What other words have "ew" in them?

Read the Book

- Encourage readers to break down unfamiliar words into units of sound. Then, ask them to string the sounds together to create the words.
- Urge readers to point out when the focused phonics phoneme appears in the text.

After Reading

- Encourage children to reread the book independently or with a friend.
- Ask readers to name other words with the /ew/ phoneme. On a separate sheet of paper, have them write the words.

© 2024 Booklife Publishing
This edition is published by arrangement with Booklife Publishing.

North American adaptations © 2024 Jump!
5357 Penn Avenue South
Minneapolis, MN 55419
www.jumplibrary.com

Decodables by Jump! are published by Jump! Library.
All rights reserved. No part of this book may be reproduced in any form without written permission from the publisher.

Library of Congress Cataloging-in-Publication Data is available at www.loc.gov or upon request from the publisher.

ISBN: 979-8-88524-904-1 (hardcover)
ISBN: 979-8-88524-905-8 (paperback)
ISBN: 979-8-88524-906-5 (ebook)

Photo Credits

Images are courtesy of Shutterstock.com. With thanks to Getty Images, Thinkstock Photo and iStockphoto. Cover – Amy Li, agolndr, Boonchuay1970, Anatolir, Nuttapong Photographer, p3 – Amy Li, Albo003, alisafarov, DONOT6STUDIO, SomprasongWittayanupakorn, p4–5 – victoras, Triff, p6–7 – AnotherPerfectDay, Perutskyi Petro, rafa jodar, p8–9 – Andrey Burmakin, Aryze, p10–11 – JIANG HONGYAN, Lena Ogurtsova, p12–13 – thewada1976, Rakic, p14–15 – AlenKadr, Chepko Danil Vitalevich, Sabina Leopa, Somchai Som, p16 – Shutterstock.

How many words can you list with ew in them?

Oh dear! Look at this mess. But we can fix it! Phew!

We can fix it with screws. Screws are long and thin, but they are not like nails.

Screw

Nail

Nails are hit into things with a hammer.
A drill twists a screw into an object.

Drill

The tip of the screw has a sharp point. This helps it twist into an object.

Tip

There are a lot of screw tops. Some have a cross and some do not.

Each turn of the screw pushes it farther and farther into the object.

Screws can go into lots of things, such as wood and bricks.

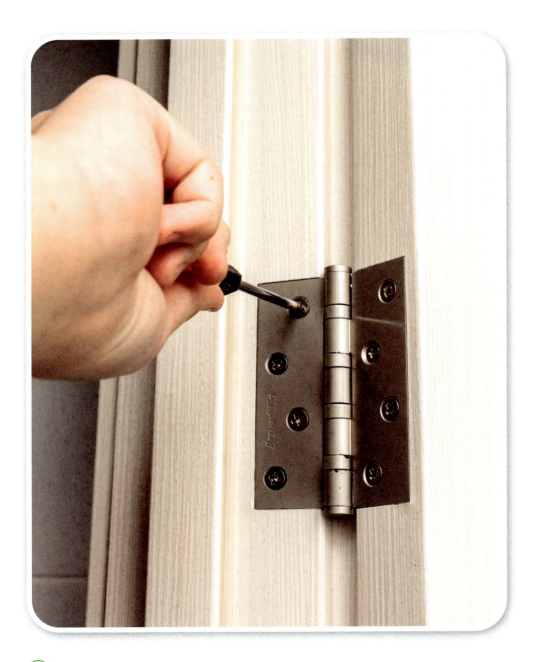

A bolt is a kind of screw. It twists into an object called a nut. The nut keeps the bolt secure.

Bolt

Nut

Some bolts can be big. They might need a big wrench to keep them tight.

We have been fixing things with screws all day. Now they look new!

Not all screws are long and thin.
Which screws have you seen?

Faucets are screws.

Lids can be screws.

Do not chew your pen cap. The lid might be a screw!

Some light bulbs have a screw.

Using the Sound Bank, trace the missing letters to complete each word.

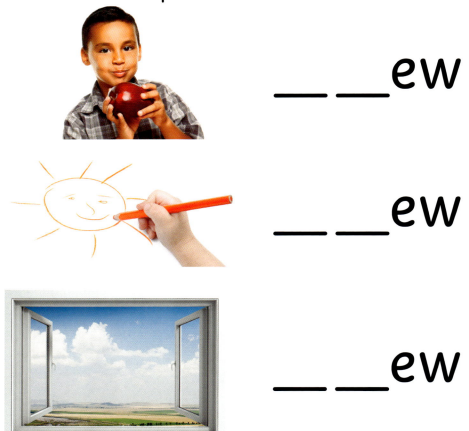

___ew

___ew

___ew

Sound Bank

vi   ch   dr